SRI LANKA

Tim Page

SRI LANKA

92 color photographs · Text by Nigel Palmer

THAMES AND HUDSON

For Eve and Caroline,
And for the people of Lanka

Quotations in the text are taken from the following sources: pp. 19 and 22 (below), *The Mahavamsa*, trans. W. Geiger, Pali Text Society 1912 (reprinted 1964); pp. 22 (above) and 51, *The Travels of Fa Hsien*, trans. Rev. S. Beale, London 1869; pp. 23 and 52, The *Culavamsa*, trans. W. Geiger, Ceylon Government Information Department 1953 (reprinted 1964); p. 55, after *The Ramayana and the Mahabharata*, trans. R.C. Dutt, Everyman Library, London 1910 (reprinted 1969) (p. 101-2); p. 75, Robert Knox, *An Historical Relation of Ceylon*, London 1681; pp. 100 and 104, *Buddhist Scriptures*, trans. Edward Conze, Harmondsworth 1959 (pp. 122 and 63; reprinted by permission of Penguin Books Ltd); p. 102, Ven. Walpola Rahula, *What the Buddha Taught*, Random House, New York 1977/Gordon Fraser, London 1978 (Dhamma Pada verses 81 and 82).

First published in the USA in 1984 by Thames and Hudson Inc., 500 Fifth Avenue, New York, New York 10110

Library of Congress Catalog Card Number 84–50340

Printed and bound in Japan

Acknowledgments

I am indebted to the following for helping me during the shooting of this book: Richard Knox at Air Lanka in London; Mr Abeysekara and then Mr Jayawardena at the Sri Lanka Tourist office in Colombo; Mr Bandaranayake, chief lay minister at the Dalada Maligawa; Thero Shri Udugodo Somananda at the Malwatha; Lynn de Alwis at the superb Wildlife Department; Louis Rasaya in Nilakarai; Primukh Fernando at Thomas Cook's; Lt-Col. Ramanathan at the Confifi Beach Hotel; the staff of the Galle Face Hotel, Colombo; and lastly Victor Walatara and Mrs Nalini Wickremesinghe at Lake House Books. Thank you again.   TIM PAGE

I wish to record my gratitude to Roland Silva for all his help, and to acknowledge my debt to Anuradha Seneviratne for his guidance on Sri Lankan folklore, and for his constant advice and friendship.   NIGEL PALMER

Contents

Point Pedro

Jaffna

Elephant Pass

N

Mannar

Kuchchaveli

Trincomalee
KODDIYAR
BAY

Mihintale
Anuradhapura

WILPATTU
NATIONAL
PARK

Kalpitya
PUTTALAM
LAGOON

Puttalam

Aukana

Sigiriya

Polonnaruwa

Dimbulagala

Batticaloa

Chilaw

Dambulla

MAHAWELI GANGA

Kurunegala Aluvihara
Matale

Katugastota Kandy
Peradeniya

Mahiyangana

Negombo

Kegalla

Bibile

Kelaniya
KELANI GANGA
COLOMBO Hanwella
Mt Lavinia Kotte
Sri Pada
(ADAM'S PEAK)

Ramboda Pass

Nuwara Eliya

Badulla

Boralanda

YALA
NATIONAL
PARK

Haputale
Buduruvagala

Ratnapura

MENIK GANGA

Kataragama

Paiyagala

Rakwana

Kosgoda

Hambantota

Hikkaduwa
Galle
Koggala
Matara

0   kms   80

0   mls   50

Preface

The early-morning light in Lanka is true magic; twenty minutes before sunrise and just after are about as close to tasting colour as you can ever arrive at. Over a period of three years, I spent nearly ten months in the country and barely missed a day's magical moments. The days began at half-past four in the morning and closed soon after sunset, whether they were spent high in the misty hills on an old colonial tea estate or on a palm-fringed tropical beach.

You always seem to arrive at Katanayake airport at dawn and the jet lag shrugs off in the beauty of your first light there. It takes less time to get from South Kensington to Sri Lanka than to get to the west coast of the USA; it even costs less both physically and spiritually. It takes a certain period of reorientation to slow down to the pace of the island, that of the buffalo and bicycle; to adjust to a time based on the art of conversation, the delight of being engaged by some of the most hospitable people I have ever met.

Every moment becomes an endless tale, the most minor incident an epic saga. My driver, assistant and friend, Asoka Navaratne, could regale me any time with an anecdote. Asoka filled me in more about Lanka than all the guide books put together; he even spotted frames that I would have missed through their very normality. Every picture tells a story; so does every Sinhalese. There is a quiet here, be it amongst the two-millennium-old ruins of the cultural triangle, at a remote shrine, or in a wild-life preserve; even when a million people go on a *puja*, there is no sense of haste, no sense of hurry; panic is a word confined to the First World. The pervading sense is that of piety, of a Buddhist philosophic calm, soporized by a climate that is blown by an alternating northeast and southwest monsoon year-round. The monsoons also provide the bounty of fish and fruit, the staples of rice and curry. Never have I felt so healthy, so in tune with the self, so open to that learning which is oft frustrated in the Occident. I fell more deeply in love with this country than anywhere I have yet experienced.

For more than two thousand years, the Sinhalese have been chronicling in the *Mahavamsa* their island, its culture, its *raison d'être*; everyone reflects a part of its spectrum. Shri Bhadra Marapana, a classic gentleman and the island's leading gem connoisseur, spent days with me at his retreat in Ratnapura, unveiling the facets of the tantric lore; he was the one who gave me the thought from the Buddha below. So gradually, as the lotus unfolds with the first rays of light, and as the pilgrim peels the same bud open to lay at the foot of his Buddha, I was reawakened to inner parts of myself and became more harmonious both with my surroundings and photographically – an earthy form of Zen. The Sinhalese are overjoyed to assist in this enlightenment; they have absorbed us Westerners for five centuries, and few of us have left without harbouring the want to return. In their century-and-a-half of rule, the British did not merely exploit, but developed and preserved many of the ancient sites and tanks; they were respected, and even today Sri Lanka is cricket-crazy. One island society blended with another from opposite ends of latitude.

It was through a set of auspicious occurrences that I met Nigel and Caroline Palmer, who had already made their home in Kandy for the past year. From then on, we were to pass endless hours on a classical veranda set high above Kandy's botanical sanctuary, ruminating over the intricacies of Lanka's beauty and intriguing past. Between here and the regal vastness of the slightly decadent Galle Face Hotel in Colombo, we orchestrated trips up-country and to out-stations in a dented Peugeot or a decrepit Land-Rover, and we would travel from Point Pedro in the far north right through to Dimbulagala in the heart of the dry zone. Number 13 Sanghamitta Mawatha, Udawattakele, became one of my most memorable base-camps-cum-datelines. And then Eve would arrive, taking leave from the world, and whisk us off to the tropical paradise of Nilakarai estate, on the beach, north of Trincomalee.

Lanka is nearly the size of Ireland, but its complexities are staggering, so I have tried to break these down into four feelings or essays. Nigel and I open with 'A Passing of Time', in which the classic sense of the island's history is explored. In 'The Garden of Lanka', we focus on the island's means of survival and growth, its essential purpose. 'What to do?' is our humble attempt to portray the *joie de vivre*, coupled with beatific and often amusing interaction between man and his environment. In 'Auspicious Moments', we express the heart and soul of Taprobane: the very *khamma* of the island, and especially the magnetism towards it that I associate with the elevating moments I have passed through on my own path to enlightenment.

For simplicity, both Nigel and I in our captions and writings have used Pali words such as *dhamma, khamma* and *nibbana*, the language of the orthodox or Theravada Buddhist school, rather than the Sanskrit (*dharma, karma, nirvana*) with which most people in the West are familiar. Names of ceremonies and indigenous occasions, as well as titles, are referred to in their native Sinhala.

Be they laymen or scholars, we hope that visitors to Lanka will derive as much pleasure and revelation as we have had working there. We also hope that they will be inspired to go there for more than a fleeting moment, to benefit from the generosity, the beauty, the hospitality of the island, and to sink in above their minds.

Ayobowan, TIM PAGE

We are what we think,
Having become what we thought.
Like the wheel that follows the cart-pulling ox,
Sorrow follows an evil thought.

So joy follows a pure thought
Like a shadow faithfully tailing a man.
We are what we think,
Having become what we thought.

SIDDHARTA GAUTAMA BUDDHA

PLATES 1–7

1   Sunrise at the *dagaba* of the Kirivehera, Kataragama.
2   Anuradhapura seen from Mihintale.
3   Sunrise from Sri Pada (Adam's Peak).
4   *Dagaba* in Fort Frederick, Trincomalee.
5   The Ruwanweli Seya *dagaba*, Anuradhapura.
6   Dawn at Aukana.
7   Remains of the Royal Palace beside King Parakramabahu I's tank, Polonnaruwa.

4

A Passing of Time

In 1972 the country known as Ceylon adopted a new name – Sri Lanka. The name was unfamiliar to the outside world, but it had been used before, both in Sanskrit and in Pali, the classical languages of the Indian subcontinent. The revival of the ancient title reflects the enormous pride which Sri Lankans take in their history, and in the unique Buddhist civilization which they developed in ancient times.

The island's past has been continuously recorded for two thousand five hundred years, reflected in monuments and detailed in rock inscriptions. Above all, it has been preserved in an extraordinarily accurate historical document, the *Mahavamsa*, or 'Great Chronicle'. The first edition of the Chronicle was prepared by the Buddhist monk and scholar Mahanama, in the early fifth century AD, the island's golden age – a history, as its preamble promises, 'of varied content . . . and lacking nothing'. The Chronicle has been frequently updated ever since, and the most recent volume was published in 1981.

The traditional cosmology of the Hindus, who form Sri Lanka's largest minority group, measures time according to the wheel of creation and destruction. Each turn of the wheel takes a year in the life of Brahma, the creator god, but Brahma's time-scale is vast – a mere day in his life equals 4.32 thousand million earthly years, approximately the same as the age that scientists ascribe to our planet. Brahma sowed his seed into the waters and brought forth life, and then, from 'a golden egg, brilliant as the sun', made the heavens and the earth.

Geologists believe that, several hundred million years ago, Sri Lanka and India, together with Australia and Antarctica, formed the gigantic southern continent of Gondwana. Sri Lanka's central mountains were the southern tip of a chain that extended up the western side of India and was then the highest mountain range on earth. The movements of the earth's crust gradually broke up Gondwana and pushed the Indian landmass northwards till it collided with Asia, thrusting the Himalayas into the sky where they met. To the south, the land slowly subsided into the sea and shrank in size, while the tropical rains washed the mountains away, depositing a layer of heavy gem-bearing gravel in the valleys below. Finally, about a hundred thousand years ago, a tear-shaped drop detached itself from the mainland, and the island of Lanka was formed.

It is not yet known when man first arrived in Sri Lanka, but recent archaeological discoveries suggest that the island's earliest inhabitants were in the forefront of prehistoric technology. Excavations of rock caves have produced finely worked flints ranging back to the astonishingly early date of 27,000 BC. At another site, a few grains of hybridized millet were discovered, apparently the result of deliberate genetic selection, with associated material that yielded a radiocarbon date of around 11,000 BC, when the last Ice Age was still retreating from the northern world. This is amongst the earliest evidence for human crop-breeding anywhere in the world. A handful of Veddah tribesmen still survive near Mahiyangana, descendants of the island's aboriginal inhabitants, and the last tangible link with the prehistoric past.

The historical period in Sri Lanka begins with the arrival of the Sinhalese, the 'lion people', from northern India, under their prince Vijaya. The Sinhalese began to settle on the island in the late fifth century BC, when the Parthenon was being built in Athens and Rome was still a small market town. The Persian Empire dominated the Middle East while in China the age of the great philosophers, Confucius and Lao Tzu, had recently come to an end.

The Sri Lankan calendar dates from Vijaya's arrival, and from another supposedly simultaneous event that took place at Kusinagara in India, where the Buddha finally passed away into Enlightenment. He left his teachings in the care of the saffron-robed monks who wandered from place to place spreading their dynamic new way. During the next three centuries, Buddhism was to expand all over northern and central India, until even the emperor, Ashoka, followed the path of the *dhamma,* the truth.

The Sinhalese, meanwhile, had begun to develop the country, and by the fourth century BC their king Pandukabhaya had built a walled city at Anuradhapura. His engineers dug out a swampy lake-bed and built the dam of the first great reservoir, or 'tank', a man-made lake which stored the floodwaters of the monsoon rains, providing a constant water supply for the capital, and irrigation for the crops. The city must have had a sizeable population, because the Chronicle talks of four outer suburbs and notes that the king had to employ five hundred street-sweepers and two hundred sewage workers to keep it clean.

Towards the end of the third century BC, a spiritual revolution took place which was to change the course of the island's history. This was the appearance of the missionary Mahinda who, according to the Chronicle, settled in a cave on the rocky outcrop at Mihintale to the east of the city. Mahinda swiftly converted King Tissa and the people of Anuradhapura to Buddhism. He then sent for his sister Sanghamitta, who brought a sacred gift in a golden bowl – a rooted cutting from the Bo tree at Bodh Gaya, which had given shade to the Buddha at the Enlightenment.

The cutting was planted outside the south gate of Anuradhapura, and the tree which grew from it is still alive today. It is more than two thousand two hundred years of age, and is the oldest historically recorded tree in the world as well as the earliest and most sacred monument that survives in Sri Lanka. Local architects and engineers soon brought their talents to the service of the new religion, and today the overwhelming majority of the island's ruins are the remains of Buddhist monasteries and shrines.

The *dagaba,* also known as a *thupa, stupa, cetiya* or *pagoda,* is a solid mound of brick which enshrines fragments of ash and bone, relics of the Buddha's cremation. The serene, rounded shape represents a sacred mountain and is a symbol of the cosmos. In the second century BC the massive hemispherical design of King Dutugemunu's 'Great Dagaba' in Anuradhapura set a new standard in Sri Lankan architecture. At two hundred feet, it was as tall as the skyscrapers of modern Colombo. The Chronicle explains that the heavy work was done by elephants, the armoured tanks, bulldozers, cranes and forklift trucks of their day. It also reveals some of the secrets of the Great Dagaba's construction. The cement of the foundations, it seems, was a mixture of stones, mountain quartz and a special kind of butter-clay imported from India. It was held together by various resins, and strengthened in the middle with a 'network of iron', on much the same principles as today's reinforced concrete.

In the first century BC, the Abhayagiri *dagaba* was built even higher, and when the Jetavana *dagaba* was completed in the third century AD, it was the third largest building in the world, larger, for instance, than any of the buildings of the contemporary Roman Empire, and surpassed only by the two greatest pyramids of Egypt. The *dagabas* represent an astonishing achievement for a small island civilization, and they are indicative of the spiritual values which governed ancient Sri Lankan society.

The ruins of Anuradhapura sprawl over forty square kilometres: hundreds of thousands of granite columns that once were part of elegant monasteries, with their meeting-halls, image-houses and shrines. But if these physical remains of the island's ancient civilization are impressive, Sri Lanka's most significant contribution to the history of mankind has been its spiritual legacy. The sacred texts of Buddhism were originally written down by a group of monks working at the Aluvihara monastery, near Matale, in the first century BC. The Pali characters were etched on to *ola*-palm leaves, and the texts have been faithfully reproduced ever since.

Sri Lanka remained a centre of Theravada Buddhism long after the religion's decline in its Indian homeland, and since Theravada, the 'way of the elders', is recognized as the purest sect of Buddhism, Sri Lankan missionaries travelled all over Southeast Asia and as far as China, where the order of Buddhist nuns was founded by Sinhalese women. Sacred texts, and Buddha images, with cuttings and seeds from the Bo tree, were sent all over the East, together with works of philosophy and scholarship, and the knowledge of Pali, the language of the Buddha.

In the early fifth century AD, when Europe was entering its Dark Ages, the Chinese Buddhist pilgrim and traveller, Fa Hsien, spent two years in Anuradhapura, studying the *dhamma* and copying texts to take back to China. The great monasteries around the capital were also centres of learning, of philosophy, science and medicine. There were twelve thousand monks altogether, amongst them the distinguished historian Mahanama, the author of the Chronicle. The Indian philosopher Buddhagosa, whose writings were to have a profound influence on the Buddhist world, was another contemporary; later, he would carry the Theravada texts and traditions to Burma.

Fa Hsien clearly enjoyed his stay, and he left a description of Anuradhapura which suggests a thriving economy. 'The dwellings of the merchants are very grand; and the side streets and the main thoroughfares are level and well kept.' Sri Lanka was rich in some of the most precious natural resources of ancient times. Greek geographers extolled the pearls of Taprobane, its ivory and tortoiseshell, while to Indians it was Ratna Dipa, 'the island of gems'. By the fifth century, Sri Lanka had become a significant trading entrepôt between East and West, where the silks of China and the spices of Southeast Asia were exchanged for goods from the Middle East and Europe – gold and silver, horses and wine.

Rice was the people's staple food, and because rice has to be grown in standing water for its first two months, a massive network of reservoirs and irrigation channels was built to supply the thirsty paddy-fields. Mere statistics of the hundreds of square miles of reservoirs and the thousands of miles of channels that interlinked them cannot do justice to the scale of this enterprise, and today the ruins of ancient waterworks are hidden beneath the jungle all over the northern half of the island, testimony to a time when the 'dry zone' was densely populated and fertile. Sri Lankan kings constructed tanks as a pious duty, and the late-fourth-century king Dhatusena completed eighteen major tanks, including the 'Giant's Tank' which faces the towering Buddha statue at Aukana.

Dhatusena was murdered by his son, King Kassapa, who went on to create an extravagant fantasy palace on the top of Sigiriya rock. The entrance to his palace in the clouds was through the mouth of an awesome lion. Sadly, only its gigantic paws have survived, but Kassapa also commissioned the charming frescoes above the stairway, and laid out the stately pleasure gardens below, with their white limestone fountains and meandering streams.

The kings of ancient Lanka did not neglect their social duties. They maintained almshouses for the sustenance of the poor, and hospitals where treatment was free of charge. King Buddhadasa was a doctor, adept in the herbal remedies of the indigenous medical system, but he was also a surgeon, who had a special pocket made in his clothes for his scalpel. He appointed one doctor to every ten villages, and set up veterinary clinics, and 'for cripples and for the blind he built refuges'.

Under the philosophical and compassionate influence of the Buddhist religion, the humanitarian ideals of ancient Sri Lanka have a surprisingly modern appeal. Against the background of the caste system, the Buddha taught universal equality; in an age of bigotry, Buddhism insisted on absolute religious tolerance; in violent times, the *dhamma* upheld pacifism and taught the sanctity of all human and animal life. The peace and prosperity of Sri Lanka's golden age, however, were not to last, and by the eighth century, powerful empires had arisen in neighbouring South India which began to threaten the island's security. In the year 993, the armies of the Chola dynasty of Tanjore ravaged Anuradhapura. The Cholas conquered the northern half of the country and held it as a province for nearly eighty years. Something of the Indian contribution to Sri Lanka's cultural heritage can be seen from the elegant temples and bronzes that the Cholas left behind in their capital at Polonnaruwa. Eventually, a powerful resistance movement arose in Ruhuna, the Sinhalese heartland in the south, and the country regained its liberty under Vijayabaju, in AD 1070.

In the middle of the twelfth century, one of the outstanding figures of Sri Lankan history, Parakramabahu I ('the Great'), fought his way to the throne. Through neglect and the turmoil of civil wars, large parts of the complex irrigation system had fallen into disuse, but he restored and even expanded it. He undertook large-scale construction projects in his capital Polonnaruwa, and he beautified the city with gardens and pavilions, paintings, sculptures and bathing pools. He also united the different orders of Buddhist monks, and founded monasteries, including the Gal Vihara, where he had a magnificent series of Buddha statues carved out of solid rock.

By Parakramabahu's time Anuradhapura was already an ancient city, and it had been the capital of over a hundred kings. The city had been sacked by the Chola invaders and deserted for more than a century, and in the words of the Chronicle, the huge *dagabas* 'were overgrown with great trees, bears and leopards dwelt there, and the ground of the jungle scarce offered a foothold by reason of the heaps of bricks and earth.' Parakramabahu the Great, 'after having the forest cut down, and the *dagabas* built in the proper fashion, and faced with stucco … saw to the restoration of whatever was decayed, or fallen in.'

Soon after Parakramabahu's death, a terrible disease (perhaps malaria) swept the island, and a disastrous series of civil wars and foreign invasions, as the Chronicle makes clear, 'destroyed the entire social structure and the religious organization'. The dams of the mighty tanks on which the economy depended were smashed open, and Sri Lanka's own 'Dark Ages' began. For half a century the land was ruled by warlords and looted by mercenaries. The following six hundred years were to witness an increasingly desperate epic of resistance to one foreign attack after another. The Indians invaded several times, and established a separate kingdom in the north which lasted for several centuries. Next, it was the turn of pirates from Malaysia and Indonesia; then, in the year 1410, came the Chinese admiral Ching Ho of the Ming Dynasty.

There was a brief respite, when the patronage of the court at Kotte produced some of the most powerful works of Sinhalese literature, but in the early sixteenth century the Portuguese arrived, followed by the Dutch, and finally the British. The Sinhalese had to abandon the northern coastal provinces of the island, and they retreated into their traditional place of refuge in the central highlands, where they grew the spices for which the island became renowned. The final flowering of Sri Lankan culture took place in the hill kingdom around Kandy, with the Temple of the Tooth Relic as its focal point. Although the last king of Kandy was deposed by the British in 1815, the arts and folklore of the Kandyan period have been kept alive.

After regaining their independence in 1948, the people's consciousness of their own culture and history became a powerful factor in the development of a new national spirit. The traditional art forms came back into fashion; young men in the cities took up drumming, and young women revived the dance. When the people voted for a democratic, republican constitution in 1972, they decided to dispense with the English name Ceylon, and in its place they chose the ancient name Sri Lanka, the Resplendent Land.

9

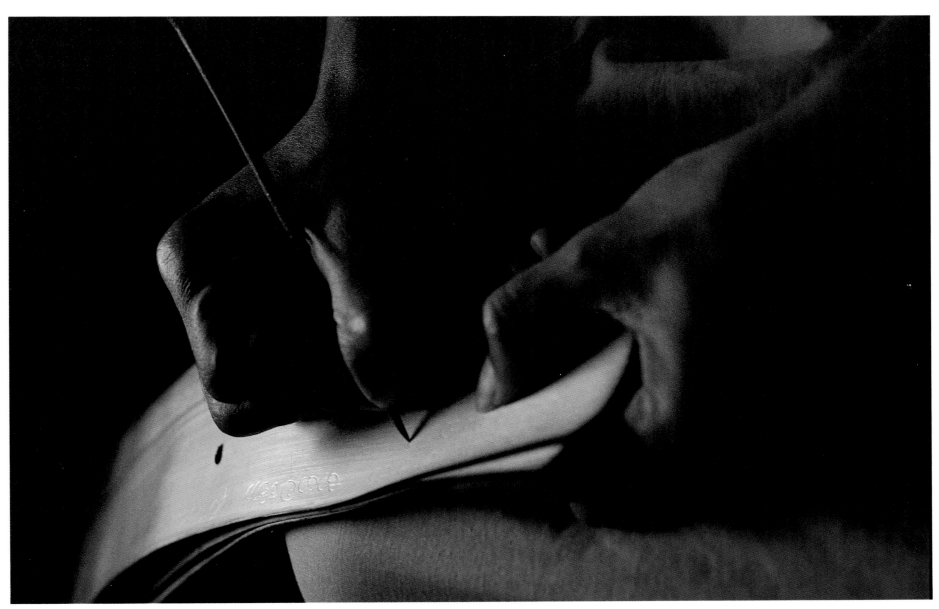

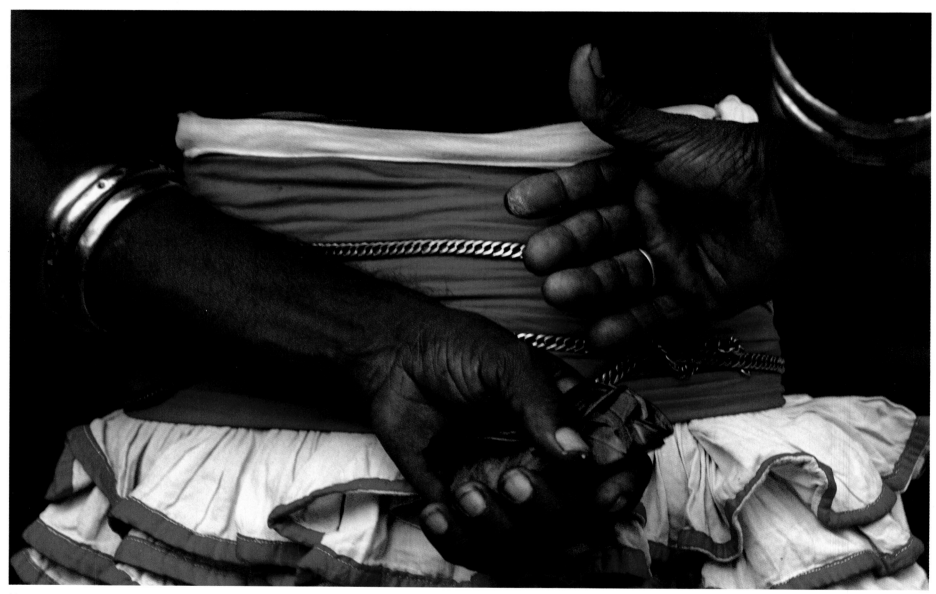

The Garden of Lanka

The pole-star is the fixed point of the northern skies, and the needle on the compass indicates north. The southern skies, however, have no fixed stars, and in Buddhist countries the orientation is always towards the east, the quarter of the dawn. I found myself waking earlier each morning until, in tune with local rhythms, my eyes were opening with the first of the light. This is the coolest time of the day, when the high-pitched shrilling of the night cicadas begins to die down, and the orchestra of the birds is just warming up. The sun flashes briefly above the horizon, but the mists soon wreathe up from the valleys and swallow it, absorbing the rays into pale-golden fluff. The next couple of hours belong to the light, changing minute by minute, casting purple shadows across the mountains, and splashing the underbellies of the clouds with lurid pink, crystallizing on the dew. It is a time when Tim likes to be out with his cameras and it lasts until the sun comes to dominate the sky, harsh and hot and white, and the day has definitely broken.

Lanka's sultry climate seems to cast a spell over all its visitors. The normally accurate Fa Hsien was beguiled into thinking that the soil was perpetually fertile. 'The vegetation is always luxuriant', he wrote, 'cultivation proceeds whenever men think fit; there are no seasons for it.' Muslims and Christians came to believe that the island had something to do with the Garden of Eden, or Paradise itself. Where else could a whole family support itself on only two acres of land?

Sri Lankans reckon on two main seasons, the two monsoons, and the rice harvests which they bring. In the lush foothills to the south of the mountains, there are places where it rains every day, but up round Elephant Pass, the salt-desert scrub has to make do with less than fifteen inches a year – and it all comes down in three days. You can drive from one extreme to the other in about eight hours, passing through a dozen different landscapes on the way.

In the beginning the island was covered by dense jungles, stocked with some of the most valuable timbers of the tropics – satinwood and ebony, white sandalwood and calamander. These have been largely grubbed out, and the trees which now dominate the dusty dry-zone jungles are the fan-tufted palmyrah palm, the majestic banyan, and the tamarind tree, which lives for thousands of years. The banyan is the holy tree of Sri Lanka's Hindus, but both the palmyrah and the tamarind were worshipped in pre-Buddhist times, before the sacred Bo tree at Anuradhapura supplanted them.

I had assumed that the survival of this extraordinary tree – this living witness to the Enlightenment – was something of a miracle, but I discovered that it was actually the result of a consistent and deliberate policy of conservation. The hereditary descendants of the original guardians appointed by King Tissa still keep watch over the tree with the chapter of Buddhist monks who have always tended it. In ancient times, the tree had its own wells and ponds and its own channel of water leading from King Tissa's great tank. At special ceremonies, fragrant earth was sprinkled on the ground, and pilgrims bathed the leaves with water in veneration. In modern times, the health of the Bo tree has become the responsibility of the Curator of the Royal Botanical Gardens at Peradeniya, and the present Minister of Culture is himself one of the hereditary guardians.

The royal gardens of ancient Lanka have not lasted quite so well. The stonework of their pavilions and bathing pools is all that remains of a unique style of landscape gardening – chaste stone architecture which merges imperceptibly into the natural flow of massive rock. If King Kassapa's formal gardens at Sigiriya are somehow reminiscent of the grandeur of Versailles, then Parakramabahu's exquisite lotus-pools at Polonnaruwa bear comparison with the works of the Moghuls. Here is the Chronicle's description of Parakramabahu's own garden:

> The ruler had a private garden laid down . . . its trees were twined with jasmine creepers and it was filled with the murmur of the bees drunk with manifold juice of the blossoms . . . Pleasant it was, and with the cry of the peacocks and the gentle twitter [of the birds] it always delighted the people.

One day I remember trying to count the number of different kinds of vegetable products on sale in Kandy market. By the time I had worked through all the fruits and spices and leaves, I had reached eighty-four, but then I came to an old man selling ayurvedic medicines on a torn plastic sheet on the ground. Faced with little piles of dried bark, bundles of roots and twenty varieties of seeds, I decided to give up. Many of the plants which we take for granted in the West originated in southern Asia. Some of them, like bananas and mangoes, seem to come in an infinite range of different varieties in Sri Lanka – and where would we be without sugar-cane, cucumbers, pepper or ginger? Amongst the pulses and beans that make up traditional curry dishes, the winged bean and the succulent murunga-pod are now being revived, their protein and vitamin contents confirmed by modern science.

But if the *maluwa*, the Lankan garden, is well-provided with the fruits of the earth, it is because the island has a long record of absorbing plant introductions from abroad. The original home of the coconut palm is in the Pacific, and it is not mentioned in the earliest sections of the Chronicle, but Sri Lankan folklore credits its importation to a prince Kusta, who is supposed to be represented on a stone carving near Matara on the south coast. Prince Kusta's achievement deserves wider recognition, since the coconut has become the backbone of the rural economy. Without it, everyday life in Lanka would be very different.

A coconut palm produces more than a hundred nuts a year in all seasons. The dried flesh provides the basic cooking oil, and the milk which is squeezed from the soft white pulp thickens curries like cream; the meat is grated to form the base of the fiery *sambol*, and when the tree is finally felled, there is always the palm-heart. The palm is also the source of the national tipple, whether fresh toddy or distilled arrack, but it provides far more than food and drink.

Coconut oil makes luxuriant soap and shampoo. It still fuels offering-lamps, but it used to be the light in every Lankan home. The trunk yields sound timber, and the leaves make thatching and fencing and shopping-bags; the fibre around the husk, the coir, is made into brushes and scourers, matting, bedding, string, rope and fishing nets; the husks are turned into bowls and spoons, and they make the best charcoal there is. From its bark and roots, the palm tree yields medicines for a host of complaints ranging from rheumatism to scorpion bite. Hindus smash coconuts as offerings to their gods, while the young leaves are woven into *pandals*, the decorations which adorn weddings, festivals and cremations.

Each new wave of settlers and colonists brought gifts to the garden. Sri Lanka's Muslims are descended from the seafaring peoples of the Arabian peninsula, who controlled the trade routes of the Indian ocean long before the arrival of the Europeans. They planted their native coffee beans and they imported cloves and nutmeg from the Moluccas; they may even have introduced the cinnamon. The Portuguese, in their turn, contributed the chillies which give the island's cuisine its vicious bite, along with tomatoes, maize and tobacco from the New World. The Dutch, with the unfailing good taste that characterized their architecture and furniture, naturalized some of the most delicious fruits of their Far Eastern colonies, amongst them the rambutan, the mangosteen and the pungent durian.

The British established nearly two thousand new species, and they introduced mass production in the form of plantations. They burnt off the mountain forests wholesale, and moulded first coffee and then tea like a vast clipped blanket over the contours of the hills. In the wet low-country to the southwest, they hacked down the Sinharaja forest, and planted endless rows of rubber trees. The plantations were diametrically opposed to the ancient system of self-sufficient small-holdings, but they were efficient. When the British left, the plantations were nationalized, and rubber and tea are still the two main export crops. The Land Reforms of 1972, which restricted individual ownership to a maximum of fifty acres, have gone some way to restoring the traditional landholding pattern, while the new small-holders are protected by rural cooperatives.

The soil is Sri Lanka's most important resource, and half the labour force still works on the land, but the second great resource is the sea. The diet is predominantly vegetarian, but it has always included fish, and the fishing industry still supports half a million people. Fishermen may belong to any of the island's main religions, but the Catholic fishermen of the Negombo region are the descendants of the first Sri Lankan Christians, converted by St Francis Xavier and the Franciscan monks who followed in the wake of the Portuguese invasion in the

53

early sixteenth century. In those days the pearl-beds off Mannar were world famous, and they continued producing pearls until the 1950s, when the oysters were attacked by a mysterious virus and all but died out. Happily, the oysters have recently recovered, and pearl-fishing looks set to become a major source of income again. Corals and shells have been exported since Roman times, but the exploitation of the coastline has been accelerating so fast that in the last decade or so, some of its denizens, like the delicious Sri Lankan lobster, are in danger of extinction.

Most fishermen, however, still prefer traditional methods, and the idea of wholesale exploitation remains alien to their happy-go-lucky philosophy. It is also contrary to Buddhist thinking, since respect for all forms of life is the first of the five precepts to which every Buddhist subscribes.

The history of Sri Lankan Buddhism begins with the story of how King Tissa spared the life of a stag while hunting at Mihintale, and it has been forbidden to kill any living creature within the boundaries of the monastery for more than two thousand years, which makes it one of the oldest animal sanctuaries in the world. The proportion of Sri Lanka's surface area which is now devoted to wild-life sanctuaries and strict natural reserves puts many larger and richer countries to shame. A number of species, such as the leopard and the star tortoise, are now officially protected, and poaching is rare; watchers use fire-crackers to guard their crops rather than guns, and their most effective defence against monkeys is sky-rockets.

Other animals, like the wild elephant, owe their protection to traditional mores. Consider, for a moment, the strange history of Major Rogers, a worthy administrator of colonial days. He was a great builder of roads and a pillar of justice, so beloved by the people of Badulla that they built a church in his memory after his death. As Lankans see it, it was Major Rogers' sporting instincts which led to his downfall – when asked how many elephants he had shot, he liked to say that after thirteen hundred, he hadn't bothered to keep the score. In Haputale one evening, while still in his prime, against the backdrop of the grandest view on the island, Major Rogers was struck dead by lightning. But the curious part of the story is this, that no sooner had his tombstone been erected in Nuwara Eliya, than it, too, was destroyed by lightning.

Since the British packed up their shot-guns and left, the birds have not been seriously threatened. They are indeed astonishingly tame, and thousands of international bird-watchers flock to the island every year to see them. I had never been particularly interested in birds, but I couldn't ignore the kingfishers that seemed to pose on every telephone wire, or the tiny, glistening sun-birds that made their nest on the veranda. When the mulberries ripened, a pair of golden orioles began to call, and I bought my first bird book, to help me distinguish the velvet-fronted nuthatch from the pompadour pigeon, the bird of paradise flycatcher from the drongo. Now I am spoiled, and the birds of the north seem frumpy in comparison. Besides, I find it hard to forget the view from my balcony, looking out over the forest of Udawattakele, with the 'kook' of the cougal announcing the sunset, and the first of the fruit-bats sliding silently across the sky.

Because no one shoots them, crows are the island's worst pest. They are such dreadful thieves that the mere possession of a tame crow is an offence in Sri Lankan law, while to be reborn as a crow is a fate considerably worse than the passing phenomenon of death. But the crow has an essential role in the life-cycle of the Bo tree, whose seeds can only be propagated, it is said, by passing through its digestive system, and so it, too, is protected. Crows, like geckos, are regarded as instruments of divination, and for those who can interpret them, their every appearance and utterance is full of significance.

The island has often been compared to the garden of Eden, and it must be said that the undergrowth conceals a fair quota of dangerous snakes, with the deadly king cobra at their head. But while westerners regard cobras with fear and loathing, Sri Lankans think of them as gentle, protective creatures, who never attack unless provoked. If a villager comes across a cobra in the fields, he brings his hands together in the gesture of respect and addresses it as 'naihamy', 'cobra-lord'. The stone-carved cobras which guard the entrances to shrines commemorate the king of cobras, Mucalinda, who wrapped his coils around the Buddha's body while he was in deep meditation, and who raised his hood above the Buddha's head to shelter him from a raging storm. The *naga*, the cobra, is associated with the Bo tree, and it often makes its home in the tree's winding roots. The rarest of all cobras, the albino, is considered highly auspicious. To kill a cobra is almost unthinkable, not least because of the tradition which says that, if anyone kills a *naga*, his family will have to pay the penalty for seven generations.

Of the illustrious travellers of the past, Marco Polo and Ibn Batuta left glowing descriptions of Sri Lanka, but for me the most lyrical lines on the island are in the *Ramayana* epic – the cycle of Hindu legends that is perhaps the best-known folk-story in the world, performed by actors and puppets, sung, recited and danced all over India and Southeast Asia. The monkey-god Hanuman was Lanka's first recorded visitor. When he came in search of Sita, he lept across the sea and landed somewhere just to the north of Wilpattu National Park, where the landscape still survives unchanged:

Herds of tame and gentle creatures in the grassy meadows strayed.
Song-birds trilled in leafy thickets, birds of plumage lit the shade –
Limpid lakes of scented lotus with their fragrance filled the air . . .
Rich in fruit and laden creeper and in beauteous bush and tree,
The flower-strewn land of Lanka, like a gem-bespangled sea.

PLATES 31–46

41

43

What to do ?

There is a month of steamy pressure which leads up to the northeast monsoon, a dangerous season, when mosquitoes flourish, and the murder rate goes up dramatically, when smouldering communal feuds can easily flare up into riots. It was on one of those muggy mornings that I was waiting my turn in the Post Office, but the fan hadn't been working for several years, and the tourist at the front of the queue had reached saturation point.

'For three days I am trying to make this call,' he snarled. 'My business is very important – please!'

'Extremely sorry, sir.' The girl behind the counter pretended not to notice the sweat that was plastering the T-shirt to his body, but her sari looked very much cooler. 'We are trying to help you sir, but nobody is replying. I think sometimes it is better if you are going to Colombo.'

'Impossible. I must lose two days to go to Colombo.' He had begun to scream, but the lady simply shrugged her shoulders and produced the classic Singlish reply:

'What to do?'

The tourist was led away by his girlfriend, and I felt I ought to make some sort of apology, so I blamed it on the hot weather. We weren't used to it, I said.

'Aiyo!' She sighed. 'Tourist-people are all this way. What I am wanting to know is – what is this thing? Why you all are wanting everything urgent-rate? You are not having any time over there, is it?'

It didn't take long to learn Singlish, but there was one gesture that I couldn't make out for months – a wobbling of the head from side to side, rather like those toys which have their heads attached to their bodies by a loose spring. I noticed that the head-wobble was invariably accompanied by an 'oh', so I asked what the word meant. The dictionary said that it meant 'yes', but it seemed just as likely to mean 'no', and the bobble of the head was the same. It finally dawned on me that both were expressions of pure politeness, signifying complete agreement with whatever I was saying. It is considered extremely bad manners to disagree with people or to contradict them, particularly if they are foreign guests.

Sri Lankans always have time for conversation, in fact, as Robert Knox observed, 'this manner of passing their leisure time, they account their greatest recreation'. Quite apart from good manners, the information exchanged in the normal round of social activities acts as the 'news' of a predominantly rural society. The British were so impressed by the speed of this mouth-to-mouth network that they coined the expression 'jungle telegraph' to describe it. A good joke goes round the island in three days, but a hot political scandal needs only three hours, and this habit of non-stop conversation may well be the reason for the curious fact that there is no word for 'boredom' in Sinhalese.

There are two kinds of Sri Lankans today – those whose digital wrist-watches proclaim that their lives are ruled by the urgent necessities of time, and those who still measure their day by the chime of temple bells and the passage of the sun through the sky, and their weeks by the quarters of the moon. The cosmopolitan élite of Colombo 7 have more in common with the inhabitants of the developed world than with their fellow countrymen who work up to their waists in the mud of the paddy-fields, and the process is accelerating, because the only way to get ahead is to acquire a Western education and to abandon the comfortable sarong for the smartly pressed trousers which define the middle classes. In the recurring dilemma of the Third World, torn between the slow-moving life-style of the village and the allure of the radio-cassette and the Japanese car, hundreds of thousands of Sri Lanka's most skilled people have been driven to earn their living abroad.

The photographs in this book tend to concentrate on the traditional aspects of Sri Lankan culture, because these are the aspects of the island which are unique. From Ulan Bator to Timbuktu, the modern world looks much the same as it does in Colombo, with its jumbled telephone wires and messy building sites. However, while the aesthetics of rural life may be more pleasing to the casual visitor, without development, the problems of poverty will not go away, and Sri Lanka is amongst the twenty poorest nations on earth.

Despite its severely limited resources, Sri Lanka belongs (with China and Cuba) to a very small and select group of Third World countries which have been able to provide a comparatively comprehensive network of social security for their citizens. There is no starvation, and the poorest third of the population receive stamps entitling them to free rice and kerosene. Successive socialist governments have ensured free education and health-care, and have enacted reforms to narrow the yawning gap between rich and poor which demeans so many other impoverished nations. Adult literacy is high (ninety-two per cent), and population growth is under control, but the most astonishing successes have been in the two crucial areas of infant mortality – which is now equivalent to the rates achieved in the mid-1950s by the West European countries – and life expectancy – where a Sri Lankan can now expect to live longer than a Soviet citizen.

Under the democratic parliamentary system that they have maintained since 1931, Sri Lankans have recently opted for a more open economy. A Free Trade Zone has been declared, and in recent years the country's growth rate has sometimes come close to those of the newly industrializing countries of neighbouring Southeast Asia. Foreign aid now accounts for half of all government spending, and the pace of development has speeded up enormously. The gigantic Mahaweli Development Scheme is taming the country's largest river-basin, with dams for hydro-electric power and enough irrigation to bring half a million acres of the dry-zone back into cultivation.

76

The women of Sri Lanka still collectively walk millions of miles every day to fetch water, but they are in many respects better off than their counterparts in other Asian societies. Inheritance customs dictate that a family's property is divided equally between men and women, guaranteeing the latter a measure of economic control. At the wedding, the bride's parents provide a dowry in the form of land or a house, furniture, jewellery or a lump sum of cash – in return the groom is expected to provide an income. Because of their traditional status, women have not had to fight very hard for equality of education and employment, and it was no coincidence that the world's first woman prime minister was a Sinhalese. Amongst the Muslim community, however, the current is running the other way, under the influence of recent Islamic fundamentalist movements such as the *tabliq*.

The economic statistics suggest areas of deprivation, but they can be slightly misleading. Most agricultural workers, for instance, are paid in kind, and they enjoy many fringe benefits which do not show up in official figures on GNP. The jak tree, which is found in almost every garden in the southwest of the island, provides a remarkable example. Jak fruit can weigh over a hundred pounds each; they ripen all the year round, and are full of protein. They are the heaviest edible fruits in nature, but they do not have a monetary value because they are hardly ever sold. They are either eaten at home, or given to the poor and the elderly of the neighbourhood. It is an old custom that, if you own a jak tree, you cannot refuse an appeal for fruit.

Economic necessity makes a virtue of sound ecological practice so that little is thrown away. After my first couple of months in Kandy, I suddenly became aware that I wasn't generating any rubbish. A man came round every day to buy up the empty bottles, and although there didn't seem to be many tins, a good tin can always be recycled into a bucket or a dustpan, or a toy Ceylon Transport Board bus. Wood gets burnt, and compost is vital for bananas and plantains. Waste paper has a thousand uses, and the Lankan alternative to the plastic bag is a neat paper packet glued together from old examination papers and government forms.

There are other fringe benefits to a Third World existence, including a sense of security from the shadow of atomic weaponry which seems to be lengthening over the northern hemisphere. I hardly met anyone in Sri Lanka who was remotely aware of the problem. The country's leaders, whether of the left or the right, have remained faithful to the principles of the Non-Aligned Movement, of which Sri Lanka was a founder member; they want no part in the dangerous games of the superpowers.

Sri Lanka's parliamentary political system was originally modelled on the British pattern, but the pomp of Westminster has been modified over the years to suit local conditions. The Sinhalese language has some fourteen different terms of address, titles which range from the highly flattering to the frankly unprintable, but it is perhaps the English word 'minister' which has come to carry the most sonorous ring. I remember once asking one of my neighbours in Kandy why we hadn't been getting any water for the last few days. 'Aiyo!' she said, shaking her head. 'But not to worry. This afternoon itself we will be getting water.' So why had there been a shortage? 'Why not?' she replied. 'Two or three days now they are washing the roads. Today morning, early-up, Deputy Minister was here for inspection-time. Now he is gone up-country, all is finish. Three o'clock is coming water – you will see.' I didn't comment, and it was left to her to shrug her shoulders and say it for me: 'What to do?'

There is an answer to 'what to do?', and that is – 'enjoy!' Each town and village, each shrine has its own celebration, and it has been estimated that there is a festival somewhere on the island every day. The shows range from massive parades like the Duruthu celebrations at Kelaniya to spectacles like the one I saw at Kuchchaveli, a tiny fishing village on the east coast. Every year the Tamil fishermen of the area donate one day's catch to the elephant-god Ganesha. Kuchchaveli doesn't have electricity, so they hired generators and rigged up hundreds of coloured neon lights and a positively deafening public address system on the beach. There were speeches and films, and plenty of drinking, and because the catch had been so big that year, they had managed to hire an ageing film goddess who came all the way from Madras to sing to the enraptured crowd. It all started at dusk, but the speakers were still blaring on the following afternoon.

Sri Lanka's biggest star does not appear in films; he is not even a human being. He is Raja, the ceremonial elephant of the Dalada Maligawa in Kandy, the Temple of the Tooth Relic. Raja is king of the hundred elephants who walk in the *Perahera* procession, which builds up night after night until it reaches its climax at the August full moon. His tread is calm and stately, and he walks on white cloth, bearing the relic-casket on his back. Raja is now over seventy-five years old, and has had the honour of carrying the precious casket for several decades. In 1961, there was a disaster during the *Perahera*, when one of the elephants was panicked by the blazing coconut-husk torches which light the parade. The frightened animal went berserk, triggering a mass stampede through the crowd, in which several of the spectators were crushed to death. Conscious of his sacred duty, Raja simply stepped aside and let them pass, preserving the relic-casket from harm. It is often said that Raja must have accumulated a vast amount of merit in his earlier lives, and he is certainly treated with as much affection as any human being on the island.

When the monsoons close in, and people spend weeks indoors listening to the unceasingly gloomy tattoo of rain on the roof – what to do? One solution is to tell stories, and most Sri Lankans have a vast fund of them at their disposal. The most enduring cycle of stories is a collection of some five hundred and fifty teaching stories, known as the Jataka Tales, which illustrate the previous incarnations of the Buddha, before he became enlightened. The Jatakas have been disseminated by word of mouth throughout the world, and while it is perhaps not surprising that they have entered the folklore of the Buddhist countries, some of them have travelled as far as the Middle East, where they appear in 'The Thousand and One Nights' and in Iranian mystical poetry. A few have even found their way to Europe, disguised as Aesop's fables, or Chaucer's 'Pardoner's Tale'. The 'Hare in the Moon' Jataka is told all over the Buddhist world, from Japan westwards, but dozens of different versions of the story have been recorded in Russia, the Middle East, the Mediterranean region, the Balkans, North Africa, in Germany and even in Finland. Here is a much abbreviated version of the Pali original.

The Buddha-to-be (the Bodhisattva) was born a hare. One day he met a starving holy man who begged him for food. The hare had nothing to give, but he asked the holy man to make a fire, and when it was alight, he jumped into it, thinking to offer his own body to feed him. But the holy man instantly turned the fire to ice, and revealed himself as the god Sakka. In order to commemorate the hare's sacrifice in lasting fashion, Sakka picked up a mountain and squeezed it till the juice ran out, and with this he painted a picture of the hare on the surface of the moon. The painting can still be seen on the Sri Lankan moon today, and according to the Buddha, the hare is a sign that will last until the present era ends, in about AD 4,500.

The daily life of the village revolves around water. In contemporary Lankan fiction and movies, it is down by the river that young men first catch sight of their lady-loves, just as it is over the washing that the serious gossiping gets done. Everyone sets aside a time for bathing, and friends go down to the water together. Around sunset, the tanks in the dry-zone are full of buses and trucks being sluiced down; elephants like to spend at least an hour a day in the water, and once the buffaloes get settled into their muddy wallows it can be very hard to remove them. In the long and lazy afternoons of the dry season, when the harvest is in, and the paddy-fields are far too dry to plough, what else is there to do?

Schoolboys have found their own answer to this question – the level surface of the paddy-fields makes a perfect pitch for playing cricket. I have often wondered why it is that the most enduring memento of colonial rule should be cricket. Is it because cricket is a subtle, wristy game, where skill and deeply plotted tactics play a larger part than mere brawn? Or is it because traditional Sri Lankan games are non-competitive, and the spirit of cricket is the next best thing? Perhaps, as an American friend once put it, it is because 'the energy level is kind of appropriate to the climate'. Undoubtedly the most ingenious and far-fetched explanation I ever heard (from a distinguished Sri Lankan academic) was based on the fact that the cricket pitch, at twenty-two paces, is exactly the same length as the distance prescribed for the meditation walks in ancient Buddhist monasteries. On the whole, I think I prefer the theory of one of my Kandyan friends, who pointed out that all Sri Lankans are philosophers at heart, and cricket makes an excellent allegory of life. One moment comes the soaring six over the spreading rain-trees at the far end of the ground, and in the next, on the slightest spin of the ball, the hero is sent back to the pavilion – dismissed – but that is cricket. Tomorrow is another innings. What to do?

PLATES 47–62

48

49

51

52

Auspicious Moments

A propitious time is chosen for the *Nettra Pinkama*, the ceremony for 'the giving of life' to a Buddha image. The statue is first completed in every detail except for the eyes, which are left blank. When the moment arrives, the pupils are painted in, and the image begins a sacred life of its own. An hour or so later comes the moment when the image is unveiled to the crowd.

Lo! Like a fragrant lotus at the dawn
of day, full-blown, with virgin wealth of scent,
Behold the Buddha's glory shining forth,
as in the vaulted heaven beams the sun.

Each different type of Buddha image represents a particular moment in the life of the Buddha, and the position which Sri Lankan sculptors have made their own is the *Samadhi*, which shows the Buddha in deep meditation, at the exact moment of the Enlightenment. Enlightenment is the goal of all Buddhists, and the only escape from the unending cycle of death and rebirth. The way to attain it is by a gradual process of self-purification, a journey which may take many, many lifetimes to complete. In Buddhism everyone is personally responsible for his or her own destiny. Every deliberate action that you take bears its own appropriate fruit. The law of action (*khamma*) is not about reward and punishment; it simply states that if your action is bad, the consequences will be unfortunate, but if your action is good, then the effects will be beneficial. Each good deed, each act of charity, each offering and pilgrimage confers merit, and as your merit accumulates, so you advance along the way.

The noble path to enlightenment passes through eight stages, starting with right understanding and right thought and proceeding through right speech and right action to right livelihood. Although it is possible for a layman to attain perfect wisdom, those who renounce their home lives and the material world and take on the saffron robes have more time for right effort, right mindfulness and right concentration. The members of the Sangha, the Buddhist order, follow in the footsteps of the Buddha, and their main duty is to pursue the *dhamma* by meditation and prayer, and to teach it to the people.

At the ordination ceremony, the young novitiates are first shaved, in token of the renunciation to come. Then they are dressed in royal robes and jewels, in emulation of the Buddha who was born in his last life as Prince Gautama, and who grew up in luxury at his father's court. Boys are often ordained as young as seven or eight. Some enter the order because it is written in their charts; if they remain in the world they may even be in danger. They are not necessarily going to be monks for the rest of their lives; they are perfectly free to leave, but as long as they follow the rule, they will be educated and fed.

The boys sit on mats and recite *Pirith*, verses from the Buddhist texts, as they bid their parents farewell. When they kiss their parents' feet, their mothers sometimes break down in tears. From now on the boys must keep their distance, because family love is an attachment to the world, a distraction from the way. Then comes the moment when the boys are taken to one side and stripped of their finery, and the orange robes are wrapped around them for the first time. They begin to recite the two-hundred-and-twenty-three rules of the order, which they must know by heart. They may not harm any living creature, nor steal; they must abstain from sex and intoxicants, and must eat their daily meal before midday. On pain of expulsion they must refrain from claiming supernatural powers and from praising death.

They kiss the monks' feet, and are received into the order under their new names. At the end of the ceremony they are given their first gifts – a schoolpen and books perhaps, or sandals, an umbrella, a fan, or a begging bowl. With the three pieces of clothing which make up the robe, these are the only things the monks are allowed to possess. The discipline may be austere, but it is not harsh. The Buddha experimented with mortification, but rejected it in favour of the middle way.

Monks do not work, because the Buddhist community looks after all their material needs; every village supports a *pansala* (monk's residence), the people taking it in turn to supply their food. In return, the monks attend all the village ceremonies and give discourses to the community on the full and quarter moon days, to help them along the way. The monks recite *Pirith* for the moments of passage, at births and weddings and three months after death, and these are always accompanied by alms-giving ceremonies. There are other rites for warding off drought, for starting new projects, for housewarmings, and for the start of the new school term, each with its own particular moment when the stars shine down kindly on the affairs of men.

In the last hundred years or so, monks have been the spearhead of the repopulation of the dry-zone. They move back to the ancient places of worship and begin to renovate them, so the shrines start attracting pilgrims, and shops spring up to cater for their needs. The monks then appeal to the government for development funds, and the roads are improved and the old tank is repaired. The *pansala* provides primary education for the village children, and from their dispassionate position the monks are able to mediate in local disputes. The *pansala* becomes the stabilizing centre of the new community.

A handful of monks still follow the solitary path, sheltering in rock-caves out in the jungle, spending their days in meditation, working out their own salvation in silence. The forest-monks are wary of the wealth of the established monasteries, and they distrust the tendency by which their more secular brethren have become increasingly involved in worldly politics. They wear dull-brown robes, shunning all forms of display, and are highly venerated by Buddhist lay-people. Since the discipline of insight meditation requires a peaceful environment, they are rarely seen in civilized surroundings.

Even as a solid rock is unshaken by the wind;
so are the wise unshaken by praise or blame.
Even as a lake, deep, extremely clear and tranquil,
so do the wise become tranquil having heard the Teaching.
DHAMMA PADA

Insight meditation is undoubtedly the aspect of Buddhism that has proved most attractive to Western minds. Buddhism has not won many converts by missionary work, but an increasing number of Europeans and Americans have nevertheless been drawn to its underlying philosophy in recent years. Some have entered the Sri Lankan orders and stayed, producing translations of the texts and commentaries; others have returned home to try and spread the Buddhist way by example in their own countries. There are now over a million Buddhists in Western lands, though this is hardly a significant figure for a religion which at one time or another has been the faith of a third of mankind.

In 1982, the farmers of one sector of the Mahaweli Development Scheme suffered through a devastating drought. Their reaction was to make a communal vow to the sacred Bo tree at Anuradhapura asking for help. To mark the vow they hung votive flags of brightly coloured cloth, on the railings of the 'wish-conferring tree'. They promised that if they were granted a better harvest the next year, they would offer a total of eighty-four-thousand oil lamps to the tree, and a magnificent almsgiving to its monks. Needless to say, the next year they had an exceptionally good crop, and four thousand of them set off to Anuradhapura to redeem their vow. Some hired minibuses and lorries, others rattled in on jampacked Ceylon Transport Board buses; some took all day to get there on tiny landmaster tractors, their trailers bulging with women and children and provisions. They bathed in the tank in the cool of the evening, and stayed in pilgrims' resthouses or slept in the open under the holy tree.

I happened to be in Anuradhapura that evening, and the scent of sweet incense mingled with burning coconut oil could be smelt all over the sacred area. The monks talked to the crowd in relays right through the night, the lamp-light flickering off the pilgrims' white clothes. I have been round Rome with tourists, and have visited hundreds of Muslim shrines, but there was an inner stillness that night, a tranquillity which is unique to Buddhism, a moment outside the rushing world-spin that constitutes our lives. In the morning, the pilgrims served the monks a sumptuous meal of rice with dozens of different curries, presenting them at the end with bottles of the smokey black jungle honey which is one of the very few luxuries they are permitted.

Over the years, popular Buddhism has absorbed a number of Hindu customs together with a galaxy of local gods. The most awesome of these deities is the god Skanda, or Kataragama, whose shrine is in the deep south. Kataragama is a terrifying figure, and he exacts a heavy price from those whose petitions he grants. Those who have been cured of grave illnesses, or whose prayers for children have been answered, must redeem their vows with an offering of pain. Sometimes they have to walk across burning coals, but the most common penitence is to be dragged around the streets swinging from a bar to which they are attached by savage iron hooks stuck into the flesh of their backs. Kataragama is revered by both Buddhists and Hindus, and amongst the million or more visitors who visit the shrine every year are busloads of pilgrims from India.

Just as Buddhism has absorbed elements from the other religions on the island, so these religions have adopted specifically Buddhist rituals. The Buddha-image, the Bo tree and the *dagaba* are all objects of worship, and those who follow the Buddha's path also worship the footprints which he left behind. Sri Pada, the sacred footprint, lies on the summit of a seven-thousand-foot mountain in the centre of the island, and it has long been sacred to all of Sri Lanka's main religions. For Hindus it is the footprint of Shiva, while for the Muslims it is the footprint of Adam, a belief which was shared by Christian travellers in medieval times, who called the mountain Adam's Peak.

Despite an exhausting climb up thousands of steps, Sri Pada draws up to a million pilgrims a year. They clamber up the mountain during the night, aiming to arrive at the top in time for dawn. As the sun rises, the shadow of the peak projects a giant pyramid out over the ridges of the mountains, a natural miracle well worthy of the homage it has attracted for thousands of years. The Sri Pada season lasts between January and the end of March, during the clear, dry months between the monsoons, and it reaches its climax on the last full moon of the old year. This is also the season when countless hordes of white butterflies swarm on the mountain. In Sinhalese they are called *samana,* taking their name from the guardian deity of the peak, Saman, and the pilgrims believe that they are born on Sri Pada and return there to die.

Women wear frangipani, gardenia and jasmine flowers in their hair at festivals and weddings, but they do not usually pick them for flower arrangements in the home. Instead, they offer them to the Buddha, a custom that dates from just after the Enlightenment, when lotus blossoms and waterlilies made of gold and beryl showered from the sky, until the ground around the Bo tree 'looked like a place in the world of the gods'. Where the Buddha paced up and down in meditation, miraculous flowers sprang up in his footprints, and when he finally passed out of the sight of men, he lay down under two sal trees.

'Supreme in the mastery of trances,' the Buddha 'ascended through all the nine stages of meditational attainment,' and at last 'came face to face with everlasting peace . . . The Rivers, as if overcome with grief, were filled with boiling water.' Although it was not the season, beautiful blossoms grew on the sal trees above the Buddha's couch, and their branches bent down over him and showered his golden body with their flowers.

The Buddha's teachings have now survived their first two thousand five hundred years, half-way along their predestined course, and there can be no doubt that the *dhamma* is the only way forward for the vast majority of a country which suffers from great tensions and disunity. In place of conflict, the *dhamma* advocates tolerance; in the face of poverty, the path towards enlightenment offers consolation, and a vision of perfection and peace in an imperfect and turbulent world.

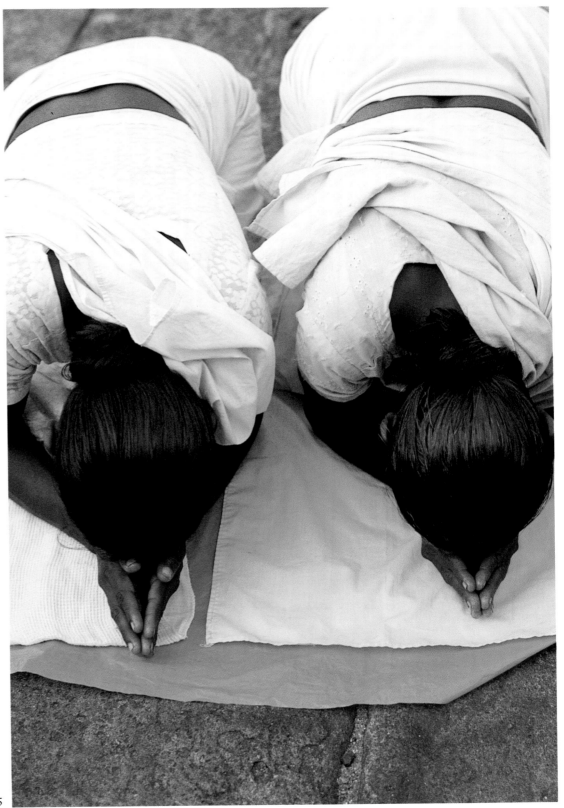

88